MEAN STREET DIA

GW01033377

FROM THE TAPES OF STEPHEN SMITH RECORDED
WHILST LIVING IN THE GUTTER DURING DECEMBER 1997

If you wonder how it feels to be a down-and-out living on the streets, just imagine.

Put on your oldest clothes and with no money walk out your front door. Throw away the key and keep on walking. Imagine you arrive in a strange town where you know nobody. When you get hungry you steal, you beg or queue up for handouts. When it rains you get wet. At night you sleep in shop doorways. In the first few days you'll miss your bed, your kettle, your TV, your bath - soon you won't even remember what they were like. Your life now becomes strictly survival as you get scruffier, weaker and start to smell. But you soon get used to it, like an animal.

That's what I've become again in the space of one week. A wild animal roaming the streets.

ALL PROFITS (20% OF EACH BOOK SOLD) DONATED TO
THE DIANA, PRINCESS OF WALES MEMORIAL FUND
Reg. Charity No. 1064238

First published 1998 © Stephen Smith

The right of the author Stephen Smith to be identified as author of this work has been asserted to him in accordance with the Copyright, Designs and Patents Act 1998.

Published by Westworld International Limited, London, England.
A CIP catalogue record for this book is available from the British Library. ISBN 0-952-9215-1-0

Printed and bound by The Burlington Press, Foxton, Cambridge.
Distributed by Central Books, 99 Wallis Road, London E95 LN.
Cover design by Sage Associates 0171-385 5069

Westworld International Limited wishes to thank BBC North for their help in producing this book and to The Burlington Press for their contribution towards the print cost.

All publisher's profits and author's royalties (20% of each book sold) will go to the Diana, Princess of Wales Memorial Fund, Reg. Charity No. 1064238.

I DEDICATE THIS BOOK TO THE HOMELESS PEOPLE OF BRITAIN

I wish to express my heartfelt gratitude to
Reverend Nicholas Howe of the Holy Trinity Church, Boar Lane, Leeds,
whose kindness gave me the strength to see it through.

Thanks to
Patrick Hargreaves and Roger Keech from BBC North,
who have made this book possible.

Special dedication to Vera Wolf, who caught an early bus to heaven.
25.7.1954 - 2.1.1998

Special thanks to my friend in London, Michael Watson,
whose hypnotherapy gave me the courage to face the ordeal.

WHY AM I GOING TO LIVE ON THE STREETS WITH THE DOWN-AND-OUTS?

For twenty-six years I was chronically addicted to drink and drugs. As my addiction took its toll I fell from being a wealthy playboy with everything money could buy to living in Salvation Army Hostels, ending up alone and destitute on the streets for over five years with the winos.

Two decades later I wrote 'Addict' my autobiography, recounting how, after the immense wealth accumulated during the bizarre crime years with London's top criminals, I finished up living in the concrete jungle, eating from dustbins.

Twenty years have passed since I was rescued from the gutter by a twist of fate when I met a young German girl on holiday in London. Today we are married with two children.

All the gangsters, gutters, drugs and drink are long behind me.

Living in the comfort of my Bavarian home I often feel I've turned my back on the addicted and the down-and-outs of England and it is for this reason I am returning to live on the streets.

In the General Election, when I stood against Frank Dobson to highlight the homeless issue I felt that the homeless were referred to as a statistic and not treated as real people. Sleeping alongside the down-and-outs will enable me to get to know some of them personally and understand how they have wound up in the gutter, just like I did all those years ago.

Parts of my stay living on the streets will be discretely filmed by BBC Television for their documentary 'Rough Christmas'.

To capture the events as they actually happen I will keep a diary, using a hidden tape recorder. The contents of this book will be transcribed from those tapes so you can share with me what it feels like be homeless.

A selection of photos in this book will be reproduced courtesy of BBC North.
Some photographs are to be discretely taken by Alex and Chris, students living in Leeds.

All royalties and publisher's profits from the sale of this book (20% of each book sold) will be donated to the Diana, Princess of Wales Memorial Fund, Reg. Charity No. 1064238

Our family home today.

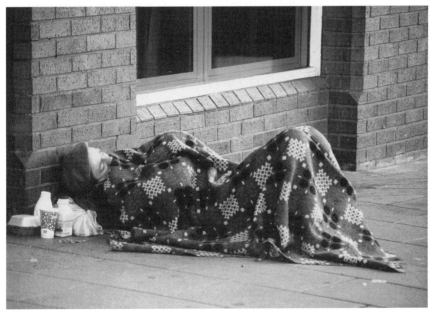

My home 20 years ago
in the gutter.

THE NIGHT BEFORE
Monday, December 1st

It's midnight and I'm home in my village outside Munich, awake in bed, while everyone's asleep. I can hear the church bell chiming. This time tomorrow night I will be on the streets.

What will sleeping rough be like after all these years? For the first time I'm allowing myself to face what I am about to do and it has hit me like a ton of bricks.

I am so scared.

This is my last night in a bed.

Should I secretly stuff money down my socks to buy food? As a recovering alcoholic / addict I'm frightened I might drink or take drugs again. Should I just carry a bottle of drink with me so other down-and-outs will talk to me?

Tomorrow night I'll be laying in a shop doorway. My biggest fear is that somebody will come up and hit or even kill me after I fall asleep.

What will I eat?

The more I think about life in the gutter the more my brain is spinning round. A part of me wants to call the whole thing off. But how can I?

Could I pretend to be ill?

In a few hours the BBC television crew will call for me to fly back to England with them. What can I tell them? I've changed my mind and I'm not going?

Daylight's breaking and I haven't slept a wink.

Oh God, I am so frightened.

My morning walk with Hannelore.

Working in my study.

ON THE PLANE
Tuesday, Dec. 2nd

8 p.m.

Flying on to Leeds from Heathrow airport.

Spent all day in London doing radio interviews which kept me busy and stopped me thinking about what's going to happen to me in an hour's time.

I'm being filmed eating my dinner on the aeroplane. Tension is building up because in thirty minutes we will land in Leeds.

Then I'll be on my own. No money, no nothing.

We land and soon after were all cram into a cab on route to Leeds railway station.

I'm nervous.

Very, very nervous !

LEEDS RAILWAY STATION
Tuesday night

11 p.m.

Lots of photographers. At first I feel a bit stupid, like a movie star. But then it's down to the toilets and as I change into my tramp's outfit reality explodes in my face. I glance in the mirror. Oh God, I really do look a sight.

The TV crew take the suitcase with my normal clothes off me, a few more photographs and them I'm told to walk out of the station and turn left.

Turning left out of the station I keep walking and realise after a few minutes nobody is calling after me to stop.

Automatically I turn round for new instructions.

They've all gone.

The photographers, the film crew, everyone.

I'm on my own, back on the Mean Streets.

Alone.

Just like it was twenty years ago.

My last meal on the plane
flying into Leeds airport.

Changing into my trampís
outfit in the station toile.

DAY ONE

Tues. evening, December 2nd

11 p.m. The scene at the station was quite moving with all the filming going on and picture people coming and going. While they were all still interviewing me I felt quite safe but now on my own, walking these dark streets, I'm very nervous.

It is twenty years since I slept rough and this is going to be no picnic. It's absolutely freezing, must be well below zero. I'm very scared, obsessed with the thought that while I am asleep someone will steal my boots, piss all over me, perhaps even kill me.

Passing two kids in a shop doorway. They are begging, obviously homeless, but they don't seem scared at all !
Why the hell am I so scared ?

Years ago pissed or drugged I wouldn't have given a shit. I would have just passed out somewhere, but roaming the streets sober is a whole new ball game.

WEDNESDAY MORNING 2a.m. Streets are getting quieter with fewer drunks about. I am exhausted. I don't know where to go but I must soon decide on a place to lay down before I just collapse and fall over. I've been walking round in circles for over three hours.

Found somewhere, an empty car park which is closed at night. Inside I discover the door to the stairs is unlocked. I go up to the top where I try to sleep on the concrete floor by the lift but it's just too cold. All I've got is one lousy ground sheet. Why oh why didn't I bring that sleeping bag?

I feel like a block of ice. This is a waste of time. I am too frightened to sleep anyhow. I'll try and find somewhere better, can always come back here later.
Walking the streets again. Feeling low, more and more dejected. If only I hadn't given all my money to the television crew I could have at least bought a hot drink. Sitting in the town square by the enormous Christmas Tree. I feel so lost and alone. My own family Christmas tree in the lounge at home seems a million miles away.

Suddenly I remember the two bars of chocolate I kept from the plane. Are they in my carrier bag somewhere?
Found them! Shall I eat them both now or save one for later ?
I'm thinking like a drug addict again.
There's only one thing to do. Eat both the suckers immediately, rip open the wrappers and get the instant chocolate buzz right now. Forget about later.

3 a.m. I imagine a bottle of whisky.
How I'd love to get pissed.
Why would any tramp want to stay sober?
Freeze to death admiring the concrete terrace in front of him ?
I'm too tired to move but I must force myself to walk on, otherwise I'll die of exposure.

Walking away after changing into a tramp.

Which way is the station? I can't think straight anymore. Every street looks the same to me.

Time seems to drag, the whole night passes in slow motion.
How long can I last like this?
This is only day one!

The weather seems warmer. No, it's just as cold but I've been moving round and my blood is circulating. Can't keep walking all night, I'll get blisters all over my feet.

Found the station, thank God. Now I can rest inside somewhere sheltered.

3.30 a.m. Outside the streets are getting crowded   again. The discos have just closed.
Hordes of kids are swarming everywhere, like drunk football crowds, all singing, shouting and pushing each other about. Will they start picking on me?

I look and feel so totally scruffy. I just blend into the rubbish that litters the floor. I feel so self-conscious, I'm just not used to looking like a tramp yet.

In the station some kids come to sit next to me and start laughing.
'Get a bath, you smelly old cunt!'
Oh my God, no. They're talking to me!

I move away onto another bench and pretend to go to asleep, praying they won't follow me.
'Are you travelling, Sir?'

A railway officer is waking me up.
'No ticket? Then you must leave the station.'
'Leave the station? But the streets are ice cold out there and I've got no money!'
'Sorry, rules are rules. Without a ticket you can't sit in here.'

WED MORNING 4 a.m. In the street drunk kids are bumping into me which I find very frightening. I must find that car park quickly and try to settle down somehow.

Back at the car park I'm creeping past the night guard who is asleep. The door to the stairs is still open. Here's the lift. This time it's down to the basement where I hide out of the way under the concrete stairwell.

I spread my blue ground sheet and lay down. It's pitch dark and very quiet. The guard obviously hasn't seen me come in.

It's so cold I hope I'm not freezing to death.
Hypothermia.
I know how hypothermia works now.
You start to feel sleepy and warm but really, you are dying.

How clearly I remember the horror twenty years ago. Stations, park benches, shop doorways.

To be back in the same cold lonely places feels strange.

Finally...........
I must have drifted off to sleep.

Leeds Town Hall where I rested
at the top of the steps.

DAY TWO

Wednesday, December 3rd

Woke up in a panic. Am I paralysed? I can't move my feet! Can't get up! What's happened to me ?

I roll over and begin to crawl out from under the stairs towards the door. I can see the street. It's still dark.

Oh no, I've forgotten my ground sheet and carrier bag so I crawl back for them. I know I'll never last without them.

In the street I'm limping along like some stray dog. The ice cold wind is biting into me, there's no escaping the cold.

Very disorientated I instinctively keep on moving to get the blood circulating. My brain is numb, a black hopelessness has overcome me. I remember this feeling so well. It was always like this during my lost years on skid row.

Trying to get back to the station to sit there for a while. Must remember where this car park is. It's in a turning opposite the Royal Mail. I'll need it again tonight.

5 a.m. Passing the Town Hall Clock. Oh God I've only had one hour's sleep!

Here's those two young kids again asleep in their shop doorway wrapped up in sleeping bags like forgotten Christmas parcels, empty plastic cups strewn all round them.

Suddenly I feel so hungry, desperate for some food. There must be some early food deliveries, I could steal a loaf of bread

This looks like a shopping centre of some kind but it's still locked. I'm cold and dehydrated.

Panic is setting in again. This is only my first morning alone on the streets and I feel already totally defeated. Can't see how I will survive the seventeen days out here.

It's the cold that's going to beat me. I just can't feel my hands and feet anymore.

Spotting a milk van I try to follow it to steal some milk but now the van's gone, vanished. Was it ever there or was it just a mirage?

I feel so totally depressed, tired, cold and hungry which makes me want to give up even more.

An hour later outside a book store......

I'm standing on an empty drinks crate, peering through the door. Two passing policemen ask me what I'm doing with the door.

'Just looking,' I reply. 'I want to see my autobiography 'Addict'!

Laughing hysterically I shout ,'I'm starving!'

'Better not push that door anymore or you'll get done for breaking and entry', says the younger of the two.

'Put that in your next book,' sneers the other.

I scream at them,

'I'm not a tramp really!'

'We know', comes back the reply, 'just got your old clothes on. Now move along or we'll have to take you in.'

Milk, milk! I see two cartons of milk outside a shop. I only steal one which eases my

Sleeping rough.

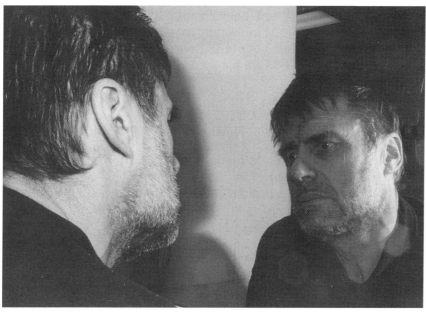

Morning wash in the smelly toilet.

conscience and I gulp it down. Feel better now.

7 a.m. At last I've found the station again. Getting busier with people rushing about, they all have somewhere to go.

I want to use the station toilet but it's beyond the ticket barrier, for passengers only. Not for riffraff or down-and-outs. They go elsewhere, wherever that is. After a furious row with the ticket inspector I just march past into the toilet.

It seems unbelievable that this is where I changed from my smart tailored overcoat into these smelly clothes only last night.

In nine hours I've become an animal.

My carrier bag is already getting tatty but I promised myself I would brush my teeth and at least rinse my face once a day. The toilet floor is wet, just been cleaned. but the whole place still stinks. While I'm washing myself a man and a woman - or was two men? - go into a cubical. I leave them to it with lots of heavy breathing and banging going on.

Sitting back out in the station I feel better now. I see the couple come up from the toilets, it was a woman after all, and now they're arguing. The man's moving off.

'You f--ing bastard!', she shouts after him. I don't think he paid the full bill somehow. For a few moments I felt better but suddenly the thought dawns on me that I have nowhere to go all day, no money and absolutely nothing to do.

A whole day ahead of me ....

No seventeen whole days ahead of me !

7.30 a.m. Panic erupts like a volcano. I rush aimlessly out of the station.

3 p.m. I've spent the last seven hours walking round Leeds just to keep warm.

Can't keep awake much longer.
Have gone into some type of old peoples dining hall by the side of the town hall.
Got no money but I ask the man if I can sit down and rest a while. He says yes.
Sitting there half asleep two hours have passed. 'Sorry, we are closing now'! A woman's voice brings me back to reality.
At least I am warmer.
Back in the icy streets all the warmth of the last couple of hours is gone within minutes.
The severe cold air penetrates your bones.

8 p.m. I begin to beg but get nothing.
I'm now so desperate for help.
It's 10 p.m. and I haven't eaten all day !

I feel a comforting exhaustion coming over me, like an anaesthetic before an operation. I'm about to collapse. It's nice, so nice to know I'm going to escape, pass out into a deep unconscious sleep.

Somehow I make it back under the stairs in the car park. Funny, I actually feel quite safe here, as if I was at home. I will call this my own private hotel........... Hellhole Hotel.

Sheltering in a shopping arcade.

DAY THREE
Thursday, December 4th

Woke up like a block of ice under the stairs in Hellhole Hotel. Looks like this car park is becoming my permanent home. I'm so stiff I half crawl, half walk out to the street.

There's crowds of people coming towards me, shouting, making funny remarks and looking at me like I'm some kind of weirdo. I feel threatened and disorientated. Who are these people? Where did they all suddenly appear from ?

I see the Town Hall clock. It's 1 a.m. Again I've only slept for about an hour! The discos are all still in full swing.

Many hours before daybreak. It's so bitterly cold. Won't last out here.

2 a.m. Sitting inside the station. Can't be bothered with the teeth brushing routine. I feel so filthy. What's the difference now! 2.30 a.m. Instinct tells me I must force myself to keep to some routine. . .

Teeth brushed. Saw myself in the toilet mirror and had a shock. I look terrible.

3 a.m. The drunken crowds have vanished. The station is empty. There's just me and another old tramp asleep in a blue anorak. He's much older than me, about seventy.

Why does a frail old man like him have to finish his days sleeping in a railway station?

A young girl cleaner is going up and down the station floor with a huge cleaning machine. If she keeps to the same straight lines the old tramp will have to move his legs in three trips time.

Every time someone comes in or out the automatic station doors open and the arctic wind blows in. Thank God at least I am not out there, that would kill me off.

On her next trip across the station the girl cleaner will wash the old man away. She will have to change course or wake him.....

Now two blue monsters in uniform are talking to the cleaning girl.
They wake the old man and tell him to leave the station. I watch as he shuffles out into the cold like a wounded dog. His old shoes are almost falling apart.

The Railtrack Monsters are coming my way now.
'Excuse me, Sir. Are you travelling?'
'Yes, I'm going down to London', I reply.
'Can we see your ticket, please?'

I haven't got one and they throw me out, too.
Outside the cold eats in to me. I keep thinking about the old man in his blue anorak. Where is he? Probably curled up to die someplace. The station guards are only doing there jobs but perhaps they're doing it all just a little too well.

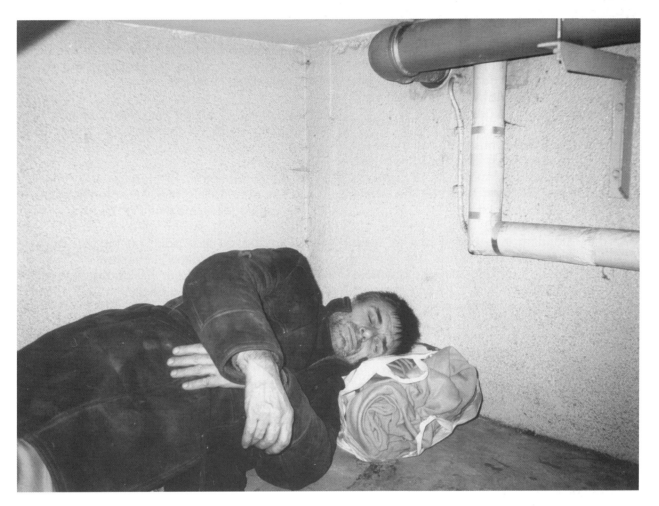

Me sleeping in Hellhole Hotel.

4 a.m. I begin to feel very ill. I can't walk about all night, just haven't got the strength. Should I go to a hospital and pretend to be ill? That way I would at least get some shelter.

6 a.m. Can't find a hospital. I've been out in the street for hours and I'm fading fast. I'm never going to make it. I'll have to contact the BBC later and call the whole thing off. I just can't take it

7 a.m. Standing in a phone box to keep out of the wind. The streets are getting busier. I'm not thinking straight anymore but one thing's for sure - I can't stand in here all day. I desperately must do something - but what?

Later.....I see a priest pulling up in a car. Now he is unlocking his church. I ask him for help. He is very friendly and tells me it's okay for me to sit inside the church where it's warmer.
Being in this enormous church on my own feels weird, but I'm so grateful. Soon I can feel myself drifting off. If only I could lay down. Perhaps I can.
Must have slept for quite some time and wake up with the church organ going full blast. Am I dreaming? Oh God, I'm going mad! Laying down I hide my face under my carrier bag.

'Would you like a cup of tea?'

There's a young woman standing over me.
'Go through that door, there's a cafe in this church. Here's a pound for a hot drink.' The church cafe is crowded with lots of middle aged people eating cakes. I'm so hungry. If only I could have one.

The priest I talked to this morning is scraping paint off the wall. He smiles at me.

4 p.m. The cafe is closing. The priest comes over, telling me I must leave soon. 'We open again in the morning', he says.

'I'll scrape all that paint off for you for a free breakfast tomorrow', I offer him.
'It's only toast and jam,' he laughs, 'but yes you have got yourself a deal.'

Back to the streets I feel weak with lack of food but somehow very safe, knowing the priest is there for me in the morning with breakfast and a warm cafe.

10 p.m. I'm starving. All my pride's disappeared and I'm begging outside McDonalds. I just don't care anymore.
Some drunk kids laugh at me as they go in but later one of them taps on the window, pointing to some food they've left.
Quickly I'm inside filling my carrier bag with half eaten chips and hamburgers.
I feel like I've won the lottery..
Won't be eating till I get back home to my car park.

It's pitch dark in here.
Can't see what I'm eating for supper but it sure tastes good.
Finally, on the cold concrete under the stairs in Hellhole Hotel, I fall asleep. . . .

Begging for food outside McDonalds.

DAY FOUR
Friday, December 5th

Nothing changes. I crawl out of my car park.

1 a.m. I'm at the town hall clock. I have only slept my usual hour.

The disco drunks seem even more threatening today. Yesterday I was told that a tramp was recently kicked to death near where I sleep.

Suddenly I am desperate to go to the toilet but there are no toilets and I haven't even got toilet paper. With no choice I do what I've got to do in an alleyway, using one of the four pairs of socks I am wearing to wipe myself. I feel so degraded, so filthy.

The homeless go to the toilet every day like this.

Sitting in the station I take off the other sock. Felt lopsided. My feet really stink now!

2 a.m. 'Hey, it's you! Let me shake your hand!' A small woman of about forty years in scruffy clothes is standing over me.
'I know you! You were on the telly the other day!'

What's going on? Now this woman explains there was a programme the day before with me being interviewed about my stay on the streets of Leeds.

It's an honour to meet you,' she rambles on, obviously stoned out of her head.
'My name's Caroline (Not her real name). Let me buy you some food.'

Suddenly I can hear ringing. She produces a mobile and she answers the call, 'I'll be right there!' Turning to me she says, 'Got to go! One of my beggars needs help. I'll be back at three to bring you some food.'
With that she dashes off through the station doors.

3 a.m. I look up to see my Beggar Queen standing in front of me with the biggest hot dog on planet earth. 'Told you I'd be back', she laughs. 'Why don't you come home with us tonight?' Her voice is so loud the whole station can hear.
I agree.

In the streets I meet Caroline's daughter, a sixteen-year-old girl begging outside the Hotel. Begging opposite is her boyfriend. A third boy, the daughter's ex-boyfriend, makes up the trio. Caroline puts us into a taxi and saying she'll see us later waves goodbye.
Home is a terraced house in Halton Moor, the roughest area of Leeds. Three intoxicated men are playing some type of stoned chess tournament in the lounge.

'Caroline said he could stay', says one of the boys. The men look menacing but for me there's a warm fire and the chance of a lay-down. A 13-year-old boy comes downstairs carrying a baby. He hands it to the young girl who is obviously the mother.

Me outside Holy Trinity.

When Caroline arrives the fun begins. She counts the nights takings, 210 pounds. 'Not bad, eh?' she laughs.

'Empty the butts,' she orders now and to my amazement all three beggars put hundreds of cigarette ends on the table. The 13-year-old is given some fag ends and with some rolling papers is sent up to his room. 'Had to send him up. Got to bring your kids up proper,' remarks Caroline.

4 a.m. Time for the real goodies!
Caroline unwraps tonight's treat - crack cocaine.

Shaking with horror I can see myself climbing back onto the drug roller-coaster I rode for twenty-six years.

Caroline orders everyone out of the room to take their doses so I won't have to watch. For all her faults, there's a good and very genuine side to her.

Soon the room fills up again with drugged beggars and chess players as I drift off on the floor in front of the gas fire.

7 a.m. The 13-year-old shows me where to catch the early bus back into Leeds. 'Off to school?' I ask. 'Haven't been for two years,' he replies, offering me some butts.

8.30 a.m. The Holy Trinity Church is already open. Inside, smiling at me is Reverend Nick Howe who greets me with the words, 'Coffee's on the table and here comes the toast and jam.' After I devoured four slices of toast in world record time he offers me some tea cakes. At last I speak. 'I should have done the work first.' 'Oh, don't

worry, I trust you,' he replies. I tell Father Nick why I'm in Leeds. He is very interested and I tell him about the years I spent drunk or drugged, living rough on the streets.

I ask him about God and am fascinated by his liberal approach to life. Here is a man who welcomes down-and-outs into his church every day. Father Nick doesn't mind if I start the work tomorrow.

Not only is Father Nick looking after me but perhaps God is as well - after all, Nick works for him!

Spent the entire day aimlessly roaming Leeds.

11 p.m. Unable to face sleeping under the stairs I ring Cocaine Queen Caroline who asks me over to her house again.

After begging for the bus fare I'm on my way. The estate seems much bigger than before and it takes ages to find the house. I ring the bell but there's no answer. Panic sets in. How do I get back into Leeds centre? It must be two hours walk away and now it's way too late for a bus. I must ring Caroline's mobile. I find a phone box but a girl is in the booth, rambling on and on. Finally I interrupt her and ask if I can make an urgent call. The girl goes absolutely berserk, shouting into the receiver, 'Joan, I f--ing don't believe this! There's a filthy tramp outside the box threatening me! Tell the girls to come round and teach the bastard a lesson.'

I'm so petrified I leave Halton Moor at the speed of light, just catching the very last bus into town. Miraculously the driver lets me ride for free.

An hour later I'm back under the stairs in Hellhole Hotel, blessing the place.

Reverend Nicholas Howe.

DAY FIVE
Saturday, December 6th

One hours sleep. Their cocaine upset me!

12.30 a.m. At the top of the Town Hall steps I realise I've lost my hat. Hope I haven' t left it in the car park. I'm too afraid to go back. There are hundreds of disco drunks everywhere. Oh God, seven hours to go before the Holy Trinity Church opens!
1.30 a.m. Must pull myself together. I decide to walk up to the BBC Studios to put my tapes through the letter box.

2 a.m. Up at the BBC it's very windy. There are no disco drunks, just a few students going home after a night out.
2.30 a.m. Laying down on a park bench I doze off but the wind wakes me up again.
3 a.m. I'm back sitting in the station watching the cleaning girl go up and down. She's got a nice bum. Some normal thoughts are left after all, I smile. There are no guards today for some reason so at least I can rest here.
I go for walk to circulate my blood.
4.30 a.m. This was the worst decision I have ever made. I got caught in a heavy rain storm. I am absolutely soaked. All my smelly clothes are dripping wet.
Why oh why did I leave the station ?
In these wet clothes I will get pneumonia !
5 a.m. Sitting in an office doorway in my underwear I have taken off all my clothes which I hung round the stair rail. It looks like a washing line blowing in the breeze. Occasionally people walk by and stare but I am so far gone I don't care anymore.
7 a.m. Two hours in the strong wind have dried things a bit. My clothes are still damp but it has stopped raining so I'm making a dash for the station.
7.30 a.m. Drying my socks on hand dryer in the station toilet, getting weird looks from travellers. Wearing these damp, cold clothes I'm cracking up. Now the bloody dryers broke!
8.30 a.m. Arrived at the Holy Trinity but it doesn't open till 10 a.m. on Saturdays.
10.15 a.m. When Church cafe finally opens Father Howe is off duty but has pinned up a large note saying. 'Man called Stephen will scrape paint off wall. Feed him with coffee, toast and jam.'
Too weak to work I leave after eating.

Spent entire day sitting in an arcade

9 p.m. Slump down in city square. A young man comes and sits next to me. 'Hi, my names Mick. I haven't seen you around before!' he says.
Mick, clearly an alcoholic, is a very big bloke in his mid-twenties. He looks like a boxer. Smiling he hands me his bottle saying, 'Here, take a swig, it's Christmas !'

I hold the bottle, trembling with fear before giving it back saying, 'I don't drink'.
'How can anybody not drink?' he queries.
'Have you eaten?' When I say no he gives me a pound. Looking at the coin I swear to keep it forever to remember Mick's kindness. Sadly the coin soon went.
11 p.m. Starving I spent the money on chips and went back to Hellhole Hotel.

Mick who saved my life.

A typical lunch on the
Mean Streets.

DAY SIX
Sunday, December 7th

Woke up extra stiff. Yesterday's wet clothes have dried on me, they're stuck to my skin.
I'm giving up. Can't even be bothered now to crawl into the street.

I think it's Sunday, but what difference! Every day down at this level is Gloomday.

My mind is just a blank.

Each day here on skid row your mind and body take a beating and slowly but surely you become punch-drunk.

Life is a survival course, you're forever searching for warmth and shelter only to be moved on.

All my worldly possessions are in a series of carrier bags. The handles constantly break, scattering everything I have all over the pavements.

After less than a week a cloud of despair hangs over me. I cannot cope any more.

I am ashamed. Soon I will have to give up.

You have to suffer out here on the streets to get any idea of what it's like to be an outcast, rejected by society, condemned to the rubbish-tip of humanity.

The rest of the day is just horrible !

10 p.m. I'm sitting in the square, having just been thrown out of the station.
I am writing a letter to be delivered to Tony Blair after my stay on the streets. I now feel I have suffered enough to write on behalf of the homeless.

Dear Tony Blair,

Ask yourself Sir.........
How does it feel to have nowhere to live?
How does it feel to have nowhere to wash?
How does it feel to have no toilet to use?
How does it feel to freeze at night?
How does it feel to sleep in the rain?
How does it feel to never watch TV?
How does it feel to have no fresh clothes?
How does it feel to always be afraid?
How does it feel to have no food?
How does it feel to have no vote?
How does it feel to have no place to go?
Tonight I can tell you how it feels.
For me and others out here in the cold
it don't feel so good!
Stephen Smith, Streets of Leeds. Dec. 97.

There comes a time when you can't face living like this any more. The depravation, the desolation gets to you.

The only escape is drink, drugs or suicide.

Midnight.

Things are bad enough for me already. Will they get worse next week?
How long can I last?
Very dejected I returned to the pitch dark and concrete floor under the stairs.

Old boy.

Young boy.

DAY SEVEN
Monday, December 8th

Woke up in terrible state! Got out the car park very quickly. With so little sleep I'm now completely disorientated.

2 a.m. Have been turned out of the station.

4 a.m. Discovered Leeds bus station, a very long, cold-looking building with rows of hard seats. Can't see any security guards. I hope I can rest up here for a while.

I don't believe it! I've found a hot drinks machine and I press all the buttons just in case of miracles since I've got no money.

'Want a drink ?'

I turn round to find a man of about thirty with long dishevelled hair. With his enormous smile and friendly face he reminds me of Jesus.

'Come and sit on the radiators,' he says, dragging his sleeping bag to the other side of the waiting room.

'We're lucky,' he smiles, 'no security on tonight.'

Sitting on the warm radiator with my hot tea feels good. Then he tells me his story. His real name is Paul but everybody calls him Macca, because he comes from Manchester. He's thirty-three and has slept out for about five months. I asked him how he finished up living rough. He lived with a local girl but they split up - she got the house. He got more and more depressed and finished up on the streets.

Macca is not a druggie or drinker, just a man down on his luck. I ask him how he finds it sleeping rough.

Macca: 'It's like sleeping in a fridge every night; you doze off and then wake up. You're so cold you have to walk about to get warm. After an hour when you are warmer you can lay down and try to sleep again.'

Me: 'What time do you go to sleep?'

Macca: 'Never till after 2 a.m. when the disco crowds have gone home. It's safer then. Less chance of being attacked. I've been attacked once already!'

Me: 'So you're scared like me! A tramp was kicked to death recently, wasn't he?'

Macca: 'Not just him, a friend of mine was murdered. This girl started taking heroin but only after she hit the streets. She was only 25 years old. There was never anything between us. We were just both homeless and slept in the same derelict building.'

Macca is now visibly upset as he reads me an article about this girl's death.

Me: 'Do you receive dole money?'

Macca: 'No address, no dole. All I have is what I receive from selling Big Issues.'

Me: 'How much do you earn a day?'

Macca: 'On a good day I sell 15 magazines which earns me about a tenner. But if you're always eating out it's expensive and a tenner don't go far.'

Me: 'Have you become friends with other homeless people here in Leeds?'

Macca: 'Yes, Mitch and Spiderman.'

Me: 'Spiderman?''

Macca: 'Yeah, Spiderman. He's got a big

My friend Macca.

spider tattooed on his face. He's very funny, loveable and laughable!'

Macca buys me another hot drink.

Macca: 'You need hot drinks in weather like this.'

Me: 'What will you do on Christmas day?'

Macca: 'Christmas day will be terrible. I have nothing except a cardboard box so I will sit alone in my alleyway. There won't be any people about in the centre. They will all be at home, eating their dinners. So I won't sell any Issues that day, will I? What will you do on Christmas day, Steve?'

Suddenly I feel very guilty sitting here, letting Macca spend his last few coins on drinks for me. What should I tell him? I'm flying back to a mansion in Munich to eat venison? I just couldn't explain

Me: 'Oh, I don't know.'

Macca: 'Come to me. We can share Christmas. We could put some decorations up in my alleyway, pull crackers!'

Macca's laughing but there are tears in his eyes.

Macca: 'Want another coffee?'

I wanted one but overcome with emotion and close to tears myself I leave him to walk the streets, alone with my thoughts.

7 a.m. Very upset I want to ring the BBC for my credit card to get Macca some money. Why is a nice person like him living like a wild animal in back alleys?

8.30 a.m. Feeling more and more guilty about not being a real tramp I go to the Holy Trinity Church. Talking with Father Howe helps me see everything in a clearer light but I'm too upset to eat breakfast.

That night I visit the Crypt, an old church where I once slept in the basement on concrete slabs. Standing outside I begin to cry as I picture myself as a young man arriving here 20 years ago dressed only in a tee shirt and jeans in mid winter! I paid a high price for my drug and drink abuse!

Before being allowed in I'm told the rules - no drugs or alcohol and after being searched I go inside. In the canteen about thirty homeless people sit about drinking tea served free of charge. Many chat in groups but some others, older people sit in silence, alone.

This is the world of the homeless. Sitting here in their tatty clothes they all have the same lost look I've seen in the missions years ago. The same lost look I had tried so hard to forget for over two decades. This is where people come when everything else is gone, after the divorces, after they loose their jobs and the roof over their heads.

Here is where they come for the handouts.

7 p.m. We all line up and are given two sandwiches and a piece of cake each. Like the others I'm very hungry and eat mine very fast.

8 p.m. A very old man tells me to line up again for more food because tonight there is lots to spare. Queuing up together he introduces himself as Tom. (I think that's what he said.) Later I leave with my carrier bag bulging with free sandwiches which I distribute to other tramps in the street.

That night under the stairs in Hellhole Hotel I feel better, not so alone now. I know Macca and Old Tom.

The Crypt where I once slept
twenty years ago.

Me with Macca.

DAY EIGHT
Tuesday, December 9th

Woke up feeling safer. Having met Macca makes such a difference. I feel I know someone now who understands what it's like out here. Walking round waiting for the Holy Trinity Church to open I met a young man who was already begging at 8 a.m. in the morning.

Tim was the most sad looking boy I ever met and looked as if he was about to commit suicide. A hopeless, dejected human being he just sat there in silence with his begging hat in front of him, someone you want to wrap up and take home with you.

I sat down next to him and we began to talk. I explained that it's not just the cold that's doing me in but also the fear of being attacked.

'Come and sleep with me,' he offered, 'I stay with my friend in a derelict warehouse near the St. Anne's Day Centre. There's a spare sleeping bag over there you can use.' Then he described where it was and how to get inside the building. Arranging for me to go over at midnight I left Tim, feeling very relieved not to have to sleep under the stairs anymore.

10 a.m. The priest had visitors and I didn't want to be in the way, so I left.
Later I rested up in a shopping arcade where I met Mick again, the boy who'd given me the pound coin on Saturday evening. Mick and I spoke at length about his life. I was shocked to find out Mick was only 24 but had been on the streets since he was 14.
Me: 'Have you been in any prisons?'
Mick: 'Yes, a fair few.'
Me: 'What do you do all day? Just drink?'
Mick: 'You could say I enjoy a drink.'
Me: 'Where's the drink money come from?'
Mick: 'Big Issue selling and ....'
Me: 'A bottle a day?'
Mick: 'Sometimes two.'
Me: 'At what time do you start drinking?'
Mick: 'When it starts getting cold.'
Me: 'Which is quite early in the winter!' I smile
Mick tells me how he was put in a kids home at 14 and life since then had been a series of prisons, psychiatric hospitals and shop doorways.
Me: 'Who knows you're on the streets of Leeds? Anybody?'
Mick: 'Well, my Mam might know I'm in Leeds; my Dad doesn't know where I am. he's not bothered. I haven't seen any of my family in years.'
Me: 'Where did you receive psychiatric treatment?'
Mick: 'Pontefract, Pinderfields and Wakefield. They gave me tablets but I stopped taking them and left the hospital.'
Me: 'Why?'
Mick: 'I didn't think I was ill!'
Mick is a warm and friendly chap with black hair and a round, kind face. After our chat I decide to tell him the truth about why I am doing here in Leeds. I was very worried about his reaction, especially

Me and Tim outside Holy Trinity Church.

since he'd given me a pound the previous evening and bought me several cups of tea and a giant hamburger this afternoon.

Mick: 'I don't f--ing believe this! I'm buying you teas, giving you money and you live in a big house in Munich!'

Me: 'Are you annoyed?'

Mick: 'No. You've got guts to do what you've done. When do you go back?'

Me: 'Next Wednesday.'

Mick: 'Right, Tuesday. I get my money and were going for a curry. I'm paying. - It's a shame you don't drink,' he added, opening up his second bottle of the day.

Later we were joined by two others but I left before the serious drinking got under way.

11 p.m. Sitting in Park Square away from the disco drunks, passing the time before I can join Tim at the warehouse.

Just before midnight I arrive to find a huge building with all windows broken in. At first I can't find my way in but then I find the entrance he'd described and squeeze through. It's a massive place on three floors with hundreds of rooms.

Everywhere is pitch dark but some of the rooms at the front are lit from the street. Creeping from room to room I'm very scared, looking for Tim and his friend.

The silence is eerie and the creaking floors give the abandoned place a haunted atmosphere.

Searching everywhere without success I narrowly avoid disaster when part of a wall caves in on me.

Panicking I shout out for Tim but there's no answer. Then suddenly I come across an old office with blankets and some sleeping bags on the floor. There are empty beer cans and food wrappers strewn about. This must be Tim's place, I think, climbing into one of the sleeping bags and soon fall asleep.

A while later I wake to what I imagine is Tim coming in. When my eyes get used to the darkness I discover the real cause of the noise - two huge rats, almost the size of cats with long black tails, eating from the old food wrappers only a few feet away!

One of the rats looks at me nonchalantly. His big eyes are cold and piercing, as if to say, 'We will eat you next!' Transfixed I just lie there, unable to get out of the sleeping bag and throw an empty can at the rats who run off.

I'm sweating now, panicking and just want to get out of the building, but I can't find the way!

Constantly falling over, creating clouds of dust, I can hear scratching everywhere. I feel like hundreds of rats are teaming up to eat me alive!

At last I get out and in the safety of the street I can breathe again.

Looking at myself in a car mirror I see that my face is black with warehouse dirt.

I practically run across Leeds to the safety of Hellhole Hotel.

Thinking about life.

By the rats.

DAY NINE
Wednesday, December 10th

Wake up dreaming of giant rats!

Early morning disaster no 1: I've broken my reading glasses laying on them. Without glasses can't use the phone. I can't see the numbers anymore

Early morning disaster no 2: There is an enormous split in my trousers. The seam at the back has come apart. If I walk about they will split completely but if I stay here I will freeze to death.

2 a.m. I am at the top the steps of the Town Hall. Trousers split even worse so I must stay. If I try to walk to the station the trousers will come apart and I'll be in my underpants.

4 a.m. Freezing to death it's decision time. Can't stay here - but where does a tramp in smelly clothes get a needle and cotton from at this time of the morning? Even if I could get one, how would I sew them together without glasses?

6 a.m. Made it to station holding my trousers. The carrier bag handle broke. Tried to ring my agent in London for advice but miscalled twice and gave up.

7 a.m. Still in railway station. Have asked several passengers for needle and cotton, but just got weird looks.

8 a.m. Went into a newsagents to borrow a stapler to get the trousers back together. The assistant told me to bugger off.

8.30 a.m. Breakfast with Father Nick. Together we fix the glasses by sticking a lolly pop stick across the bridge with black tape but he's got no needle and cotton so I leave to beg outside a shopping centre for needle and cotton money.

10 a.m. There's a long queue in the departmental store before I can pay for needle and cotton. I stink and get very odd looks.

11 a.m. I'm sitting in my underpants in a shopping arcade, sewing my trousers. Now the cotton breaks. Shit, I lost the bloody needle threader!

Imagine a scruffy tramp in underpants approaching various shoppers to thread his needle. Many refuse, shaking their heads and walking off, thinking this can only be a candid camera stunt. Mission complete, I'm wearing the trousers again.

2 p.m. Visit the Big Issue offices who can't give me magazines in spite of the fact I have no money. They explain I must prove I'm homeless. The other vendors are very friendly, which is nice.

6 p.m. Alone at the station I get very depressed.

'Hello! You look sad!' I look up to see the smiling face of one of the Big Issue sellers I met earlier on. His name is Bill Lord and it's his words that pull me together.

'Be my guest next Tuesday,' he invites me.

'Where?' I ask, baffled.

'At the Big Issue Christmas Party,' he continues. 'Just turn up and say you are the personal guest of Bill Lord and you are in - and what's more! In the Big Issue offices is a Christmas Card waiting for you. I didn't know where to find you.'

Bill's name that night was added to the list of Mark, Tim, Macca, Old Tom and Father Howe. He gave me the faith to endure another night in Hellhole Hotel.

Bill Lord.

DAY TEN
Thursday, December 11th

Waking up I instinctively know something's going horribly wrong. I'm cracking up.
I just cant cope anymore !
1 a.m. Cannot face walking the bloody streets for seven hours till the Holy Trinity Church opens.
2 a.m. I'm going to put a brick through a shop window, get arrested and get some proper sleep in a police cell, perhaps even a meal.
I have a better idea, I'll break into the Church and rest there. Father Howe will understand.
I run to the church in a hysterical state to find the doors are so thick I'll never break in.
3 a.m. After calming down I'm glad I didn't betray Father Howe.

Now I begin a six-hour ritual of walking backwards and forwards from the church to the station to sit down until guards move me on each time. I'm cracking up, crying in the street.
8.30 a.m. When the priest arrives I'm shaking. I'm too ill for breakfast, I just need some rest. Father Howe puts a few chairs together by a hot radiator near the altar and we pray together till I sleep.
2 a.m. I wake after 5 hours. The priest has gone so there's no tea and toast today.

I ring my London agent who suggests I go to a local Alcoholics Anonymous meeting.

'Worstways you will get a cup of tea and some biscuits', he reassures me.
Ringing the BBC Studios the producers sense my state and suggest I visit them. I'm so disorientated, the fifteen minute walk takes me over an hour and I arrive feeling even worse.
4 p.m. At BBC I sit mesmerised, watching part of the documentary filmed in Germany, showing my wife and children decorating our family Christmas Tree.

It's all so confusing. Here I am in the filth of the alleyways with Macca, Tim, Bob, Mick - all of us stinking, hungry or drunk. I've really become one of them. It's got so bad, I forgot my family even existed and that tomorrow is my son's birthday. Julian will be twelve and I'm very upset.
I can't go on. I'm going mad. I can't face another night under those concrete stairs!
My agent left a message at the BBC reception with the address of the AA-meeting and a 10 p.m. appointment to be interviewed from a phone box by the James Whale Talk Radio Show.
It's weird. Here I am, a tramp, dropping with exhaustion from lack of sleep, being interviewed on National Radio! I'll be having tea with the Queen next!

6 p.m. I'm walking to the AA meeting where I'm greeted by a member who stares at me in my smelly clothes.
'Hello, first time in AA?' he asks .
'No', I reply, 'I've been coming for ages.'
Looking at me with total disbelief he asks, 'New to Leeds, are you?

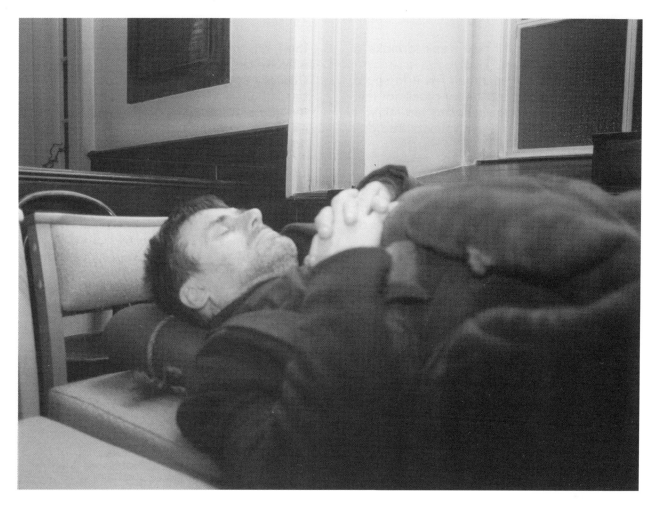

Me sleeping in the church by the radiator.

'Oh, I'm just here till next week to make a film and write a book,' I reply.

'Yeah, yeah,' he mumbles, as if to say a loony bin would be a better place for me.

'I've got to leave the meeting ten minutes early for an interview on National Radio,' I ramble on.

'Oh, that's okay,' he says.

'Just sit over there. I'll get you a cup of tea.'

I left the meeting early with several strange looks but the few handshakes I got was all the encouragement I needed.

10 p.m. Cold and hungry I arrive in a phone box to find the James Whale interview is delayed one hour.

10.05 p.m. It's Pizza Time! The night before a drunk told me how I could get a free pizza. Ring a certain shop. Order pizza giving false address. Exactly eight minutes later ring to cancel order. 'They don't keep the old pizzas ', he explained, 'they throw them in a skip behind the shop.' Well, there's a skip, so this must be the shop. Ringing up I order a pizza with extra ham and cheese, giving a false address. When the shop asks for my name I answer, 'James Whale', the first name that comes into my head.

From the phone box here I can see the ovens in the shop clearly. After what seems like the magical eight minutes I can see my pizza come out.

I ring to cancel.

Now I'm watching the skip.

Nothing. Nobody moves. No pizza.

Then, like a mirage, the James Whale Pizza is thrown out the back.

Casually I go over to the bins and low and behold! There it is!

The 'James Whale Super Deluxe Pizza'.

I eat the pizza so fast, I'll never know if it had the extra ham and cheese or not.

11 p.m. Back in town square opposite Queens Hotel I'm reconnected to the James Whale Studio for my interview. Tonight the streets are packed with disco drunks. James Whale interviews are always a two way banter and when I tell him about a tramp being kicked to death he jokes that it would be wonderful publicity for my book 'Addict' if I was killed. Jokingly I reply, 'Yes, but it's too cloudy tonight and I wouldn't be able to look down from heaven to check the sales figures.'

Moments later two or three drunks waiting to make a call pull me from the booth, throw my carrier bag on the floor and kick it like a football. 'Let's play tramp-football' one of them shouts and knocks me down. Laying on the pavement I prepare for the worst when suddenly Mick appears.

'F- -k off, or I'll kill the lot of you!', he shouts, waving a bottle, and all three run away. Then Mick takes me over to a bench and sitting me down says, 'Don't worry. I'll always look after you, you'll be safe. You will get back to you wife and kids in Germany alive.'

In Hellhole Hotel that night every little noise frightens me. Are the disco drunks coming for their revenge?

Sleeping in the station.

Cold hands.

DAY ELEVEN
Friday, December 12th

Still paranoid and the usual block of ice I crawl out of the car park with eight hours to go before I'm due to meet Cheryl Stonehouse, a reporter from the Daily Express who is coming to Leeds to write an article about me.

1 a.m. Now the mental flash-backs kick in. I was once nearly beaten to death with a baseball bat and the horror never left me. For years I woke at night seeing that bat raining down on me. Now I feel as if those drunks are characters from my past.

Is Cheryl Stonehouse part of the conspiracy? Is Father Nicholas Howe in on the act?

That's what eleven days with just one hour of sleep do to you. Like Chinese water torture it makes you believe the entire world is against you.

Walking to the station everybody I pass seems to be looking at me, talking about me. I believe today I'm going to get killed.

9 a.m. In the Station the Railtrack Monsters pounce on me as I wait for Cheryl.
'I'm waiting for the Daily Express,' I tell the guard who laughs saying, 'The News of the World's interviewing me.' As we still speak Cheryl arrives and suggests we go to her friend's house in Leeds to conduct the interview. Still convinced I'm about to be killed I get into a car with Cheryl. We arrive at a smart house in a suburb where I'm ushered inside, a normal family home where normal people live normal lives.

Looking at Cheryl I want to put my arms around her and cry. How could I ever think she was mixed up with those brutal gangsters from my past?

Nervously I sit in this kitchen, watching as Cheryl prepares a hot breakfast for me, the first cooked food I've eaten for eleven days. On the table is a bowl of fruit which seems so strange, I can't get my eyes off it.

Why isn't anyone stealing an apple? I think. How can this beautiful food just sit there ?

If Macca, Tim, Mick or the other down-and-outs could see this fruit they would eat it up in seconds. Had I already forgotten what fruit looked like?

We are about to start the interview and I ask to use the toilet which is upstairs.

It's such a nice family bathroom I start crying. I want to get Macca, Mick, Tim, all of them, cuddle them, give them all fruit to eat and a hot bath.

I look in the mirror. Is this me? My eyes look so different. I try to smile but I can't. I can't even force a smile. My heart is with my friends in the gutter and I feel so guilty about being here in this house. Why aren't they with me? Downstairs Cheryl is ready to begin. Oh God, she has a copy of Addict on the table. She knows my past - can she forgive me ?

The interview begins.

We talk for hours and I feel safe. Cheryl understands all the pain and hurt that has surfaced again as a result of me living back on skid row.

Tim alone.

Close to tears I point to 'Addict'. 'It is all in there,' I say.

Cheryl is one special woman, a very rare person who seems to understand me to the very core. This woman with her warmth is becoming my therapist, she's no longer just a newspaper reporter.

When I go back to the bathroom I cry and cry.

F--ck , When my drug roller coaster stopped here in Leeds twenty years ago I was so hurt, so heartbroken, so desolate, so alone.

All the pain of the past is flooding back like some tidal wave and I just can't stop crying.

Eventually I compose myself enough to go back downstairs.

'Would you like a bath before you go back to the streets?' Cheryl enquires.

'Oh no,' I say, 'I'm here for people like Macca, Mick and Tim. They ain't got no baths, no fruit bowls. I must go back to them.'

We take a cab to the centre of Leeds but as I am about to get out I suddenly feel so helpless. I can't face sleeping on the concrete under those stairs again. I want to stay with Cheryl. I felt safe with her.

Seconds later I watch her cab vanishing round the corner. For a few moments I felt Cheryl has ditched me, abandoned me just like all the others once did.

In seconds I'm paranoid again and decide to go to AA in the Roundhay Wing at St. James Hospital but can't find the bus stop.

Anyhow, I haven't even got the fare.

'Are you lost?' a scruffy old man asks me. It's Old Tom, the man from the Crypt.

Smiling, he puts his hand in his pocket and gives me a sweet and 70p. 'That's your bus,' he says, pointing.

I look back to see my old man waving to me. So many tramps are looking after me and I've got a big house to live in!

I arrive two hours early. The meeting is in the psychiatric ward and I'm told to wait in the lounge.

Weird people keep passing by. A nurse stops and asks me if I'd had my medicine. 'No, I'm the man from the TV,' I reply.

The psychiatric wing is like getting into a time machine going back twenty years to those locked institutions I rember so well.

When do I get my new dose of Electric Shock treatment?'

To convince myself this is not for real I try to focus in on my life in Munich, our dogs and the tree we were planting in our garden.

8 a.m. The Alcoholic Meeting begins.

I feel slightly better but very nervous about sleeping under the stairs tonight, still irrationally convinced every disco drunk is out to kill me.

10 p.m. I ask the security guards at the general hospital if I could sleep in the waiting room but I'm not allowed in.

I walk back to Leeds centre.

Passing the town square all disco drunks look like the three who attacked me. Back under the stairs I frightened out of my life.

What if someone followed me?

By a waterway.

Putting on more socks.

DAY TWELVE
Saturday, 13th December

Woke up dreaming crowds of people are standing over me shouting, 'You can't sleep in our car park!'

1 a.m. Sat in Park Square scared to go anywhere because at weekends the disco drunks are out with a vengeance.

5 a.m. Streets seem quieter so I move to the station, afraid even of my own shadow.

8.30 a.m. Outside the Holy Trinity I realise it is Saturday and Father Howe will not be there. I suddenly remember that Lucy Johnston from the Observer newspaper is coming to interview me and will meet me at the station. Worstways I will get a sandwich, I think to myself.

10 a.m. When Lucy, the Observer reporter arrives we go off to talk. She is an extremely attractive girl with long blonde hair and for the next two hours she fires questions at me. Lucy has a great deal of sympathy and understanding for homeless people and a keen knowledge of all the problems involved. She is a genuine person who really cares for the homeless.

1 p.m. The interview is over. I go with the paper's photographer, a chap called Tim, for pictures down by the canal.

2 p.m. On my own again. Oh, what am I going to do all day?! I am no longer thinking logically.

I want to find Mick and get drunk, I just want out.

6 p.m. Begging I raise three pounds and feel very tempted to buy beer.

8 p.m. I phone my best friend Michael Watson in London who rings me back in the call box. Sensing I am in a bad, bad way he offers immediately to come to Leeds. We speak for an hour which calmes me down. Michael's hypnotherapy is working even over the phone.

9 p.m. Spent begging money on food. Sat in McDonalds for hours. Felt dizzy.

11 p.m. Unlike every other night where I just climbed over the wall into Hellhole this night was different. I just stood outside in the street, crying hysterically.

'I can't sleep in there, not again !
I can't !
I just can't !'

That night Hellhole Hotel closed forever.

With my carrier bag I trudge off towards the station, exhausted from the combined effect of all my days sleeping rough.
I stink, I am hungry and now probably at my lowest ebb.

I sit in the square opposite the station with drunks staggering by me on either side as they make their way into the two big discos nearby. I can't face Hellhole or the giant rats, but to stay in the firing line of the disco drunks is suicide.

Suffering on the streets.

Social gathering on
the Mean Streets.

Should I hide in a toilet cubical inside the station?

Not looking properly I am nearly run down crossing the road by the Queens hotel.

God help me, I pray as I enter the station expecting the guards to throw me immediately back out.

Seconds later God helps.

'Hey, let me look at you! I saw them filming you!' a good-looking man of about thirty approaches me.

'My name's Simon,' he goes on to say, 'I'm working here as a night watchman.' He points to three covered market stalls behind him. 'These stalls are in the station till Christmas and I guard them at night', he explains.

'Want a cup of tea?' he invites me behind the stalls. 'Here, sit down and have a warm-up.' There's a small electric blow heater going full blast. Hot tea and a fire in the middle of that cold station. This feels like heaven.

'It's all right, they can't move you on. My governor rents this space from Railtrack so anybody can sit here with my permission.'

'He's my guest!' he shouts out to the two guards that turned me out night after night. They just glare back without saying a word.

'Saw you filming. What are you doing?'

Sipping my hot tea I tell him the whole story, including how I'd just cracked up outside Hellhole Hotel.

'Sleep here, mate' he smiles, pointing to one of the stalls, 'nobody will ever know you're under there.'

Simon gives me another tea and tells me about himself. Nightwatches are long and lonely so he's glad of someone to talk to. He is thirty, single and a compulsive gambler, although he wouldn't admit he had a problem with it.

As a recovering alcoholic / addict I am very interested to hear the story where he was going to buy a new stereo with 600 pounds in his pocket. He knew exactly what he was going to buy and where from and the money he had with him even covered his cab fare home. At the local station he just missed his train and went across to the betting shop for a cup of tea. 'Had no intention of having a bet' he assured me. 'Bought a tea and sat down. Then I got a bit bored, so I put two pounds on first race. It lost, so I had a fiver on the next.'

Two hours later he left the betting shop without a penny.

It sounded to me much like the drinker who just pops in for a quick pint but finishes up paralytic, asking himself the next morning how it could have happened.

'Addictions are all the same. Read my book 'Addict,' I tell him. 'It's the first bet that does the damage.'

I'm falling asleep listening to Simon talking.

'Hey, you better go to kip. Your eyes are closing,' he says.

So I bid Simon goodnight and spread my blue ground sheet under one of the stalls. I feel safe in my new luxury hotel.

Hotel Station Floor.

Rest time on the Mean Streets.

DAY THIRTEEN
Sunday, December 14th

Woke up on the station floor under the market stall to hear the 6.15 train was leaving from platform seven.

This meant I had slept longer that night than the rest of the week put together. Knowing subconsciously I was not going to be kicked to death coupled with sheer exhaustion allowed me those extra hours rest.

Soon I was to discover there was a price to pay.

My kidneys !

Whereas in Hellhole Hotel I had been on the concrete floor for only one hour. I had had slept for six on the station floor in the constant draught from the automatic doors.

'I slept great,' I said, greeting Simon, my new landlord.

'I'm glad you did,' he replied, looking tired at the end of his 12 hour shift.

'Here, you might need this,' he said, giving me two pounds.

8.30 a.m. I went to the Holy Trinity Church and sat in the outer room. Physically I felt quite ill now, I didn't even eat breakfast. The pains in my kidneys were getting worse and I decided to keep warm today.

11 a.m. I meet Tim begging outside the Church. Somehow today I want to come clean with everybody and sitting down in the street I tell him my whole story. At first he seems confused as to what I'm doing in scruffy clothes if really I was rich. But after a while he smiles and says, 'I still like you and I'm glad we met.' I leave him begging and walk over to the St, Anne's Day Centre. I have to keep my kidneys warm.

At St. Anne's I drink several teas but can't face eating anything. This centre is run extremely well, it's one of the best places I have ever seen. When a tramp first comes in they give him a few days free credit on food, nobody ever goes hungry. The staff there are second to none, very dedicated people who get involved with everybody that comes by. That day I sit and watch TV with two older guys who just stare into space. They're not interested in the program. Life at this low level is very hard and it depresses me to see people so lost, especially the old.

3.00 I bump into Macca and we go into McDonalds together. I tell Macca the truth about myself, expecting him to reject me, but quite the opposite. He's now even more friendly.

'Great!' he said. 'Two children. That's just great.' I was really amazed about how much this man cared for me.

8.00 p.m. I feel so ill I must rest so I go to the station to ask Simian if I can lay down under the stalls.

'It's a bit early, but if no one sees you, it's all right by me, mate,' he replies.

First I warm my back by his heater but it doesn't really help a lot. Wearing all my spare pullovers I lie down and pass out with sheer exhaustion.

Woman in St. Anne's Day Centre.

DAY FOURTEEN
Monday, December 15th

Wake on station floor. It's 3 a.m. and my kidneys hurt worse.

4 a.m. I am very restless, worried about the pain and with the two pounds Simon gives me I decide to walk to the bus garage to use the hot drinks machine and perhaps sit on the radiator.

5 a.m. The radiator at the bus station is full-up, no more sitting space available. This low radiator, about two feet off the floor, makes the perfect seat for cold tramps - security permitting, that is. That morning there were five tramps sitting on it warming their bums.

I get talking to two of them, a man of 49 called Ronny from Scarborough and his mate Richard 41 from Dewsbury. Both nice chaps but mentally worse for wear after a long period of roaming the country, living rough. They only recently arrived in Leeds.

6 a.m. I go to the toilet somewhere by the arches and must have passed out because the next thing I remember is laying on my back, staring at hundreds of pigeons all gathered together on a roof. A car is parking close to me. I feel bad. What is a dormitory for winos at night turns into a car park the next morning.
These arches are just being used by different people for different reasons.

8.30 a.m. Sitting on the steps of my church praying that Father Howe arrives soon.

I sleep for hours in the Church.

Wake up hearing a service going on, Father Howe is praying for the homeless.
9 p.m. That evening as I'm walking back to the station I come across Macca slumped in a doorway.
'What's up?' I enquire.
'Oh, just a bad run. Haven' t sold an Issue or eaten all day, have you?' he asks.
As we are talking a parcel is dropped off at his feet, labelled, 'Compliments of Leeds Postal Service'.

Macca rips it open to find a bottle of wine, some type of deodorant, a bag of toffees and a Swiss roll.
He devours the toffees like a starving man.

When he offers me the last one I take it.
Macca then brakes open the Swiss roll and dividing it offers me half.
I refuse but ask him for the empty packet on which I later write the following:

'Don't ever forget. This man offered you half of all he had in the world and he hadn't eaten all day.'

That Swiss roll packet is now framed on my office wall.
For me Macca is one very special person!

10 p.m. The cold! My kidney pains are more severe than ever.
11 p.m. Going to sleep under Simon's market stall in the station. He's bought my book in the local Waterstones and is full of questions but I'm too ill to talk.

Macca giving me half his Swiss roll, half of all he had in the world.

DAY FIFTEEN
Tuesday, December 16th

1 p.m. I wake up on the station floor very worried. The pain is much, much worse. At first I sit with Simon by the blow heater but every time the station doors opens the draught cuts through my clothes so I decide to walk about to keep warm.

On the way to the bus shelter I'm approached by a young girl who can't be more than 13 years old. 'Want a blow-job?' she asks. What kind of life has this kid got ahead of her or behind her, for that matter? I cross the road to avoid talking to the child and watch her approach other passers-by.

Moments later I myself am approached by another girl in her early twenties. 'Want to come back to my place for a good time?' she propositions me. Is she kidding, I ask myself? I look and smell like a dirty tramp! 'Come on,' she says, 'you can do what you like with me for twenty quid.' 'Is your place warm?' I ask, thinking if I she lets me pay her with the two phone cards I got from the Observer reporter, I could at least keep my kidneys warm until the church opens. I offer both cards, saying 'I don't want any sex, let's just talk.' 'Dirty talk costs the same, take it or leave it,' she replies.
Pausing she asks, 'Aint you got no rings or watches?'
All I've got is the small gold medallion my wife tied round my neck for luck before I left Munich. But I feel so ill now I need the warmth at all costs. It looks like snow.

Finally she agrees to let me stay till morning and we settle on a deal for both phone cards and the medallion.

She takes me to a nearby cab rank where I'm told to wait while she talks to various drivers before beckoning me over.

Off we drive until the cab stops in a poor part of town outside an old terraced house. Again I'm told to wait in the garden while the driver and girl go inside. Literally five minutes later the driver, looking dishevelled, reappears and hastily leaves.

When the girl waves me inside she says, 'Sorry, Love. Had to work off the fare with the driver.'

Pointing to a gas fire going full blast she proudly says, 'I don't lie,' and putting her hand out demands, 'cards and necklace.'
I pay her and telling her part of my story, drift off into a deep sleep by the gas fire.

About six hours later I wake up to find my hostess out for the count fully dressed on the bed nearby. The gas fire is still on.

'Kept the fire on all night for you, didn't I?' she smiles, waking up. 'How far are we from town?' I want to know. 'Twenty minutes', she replies, 'you can catch the bus near the corner down the road.' She gets up and leads me out of her bedsit down to the front door.
'Here, Love, there's a pound for your fare. 'Take your necklace. Please give it back to

My friend Steve.

your wife tomorrow. My brother's on drugs out there somewhere. Perhaps what you do will help him one day.'

An hour later I was by the ever hot radiator in the Holy Trinity Church, feeling excited by now, knowing that this was my last day. Father Nick congratulated me, joking, 'Extra tea cake today!'
We talked for ages about my stay in Leeds and how it had affected me both physically and mentally.

Another down-and-out, a man of about thirty, came in the cafe. I had regularly seen this chap in here or sleeping at the back of the church. The previous day I had given him thirty pence left over from Simon's two pounds.
He always just stared at me and we never really spoke but he could clearly overhear the conversation I had with the priest.
Later the man left the cafe and sat on one of the low chairs at the back of the church like he always did.
As I pushed the chairs together at the front by the altar he came up to me and said,

'Going home tomorrow, are you?'

'I'm sorry,' I said, as if to apologise for not being a tramp.

He didn't reply.

Having lived as I once did in the streets, on park benches, I knew how he felt. He himself was going no place. But I was to be released from the prison of skid row.

I stayed in the church most of the day to keep out of the cold. The weather was freezing again with snow expected.

8 p.m. That evening I was due to go to the Big Issue Christmas party to meet Bill. I walked around Leeds for hours looking all over for the pub but after trying many places gave up. I was very upset because I didn't want to let Bill down.
Sorry Bill!

I got to the station early to find a smiling Simon waiting for me with a million questions about my biography 'Addict' which he'd read all day. Simon and I had by now become good friends and along with Suzie, the station cleaner, we sat round the blow fire, talking for hours.

I kept thanking Simon because I knew without his help over those last three nights I would have had a breakdown.

I had reached a point where I could not take the pitch dark of Hellhole Hotel any more.

'Think nothing of it, mate,' he replied with his usual friendly smile.

Tonight was my last night sleeping out in the open. It seemed unbelievable but this time tomorrow I would be in a warm bed with my wife, I thought to myself.

'You'll have a right kiss and cuddle tomorrow!' smiled Simon as I crawled under the market stall for the last time.

Mean Street Shadow.

DAY SIXTEEN
Wednesday, December 17th

2.00 a.m. I'm waking up on the station floor. I feel very excited and quite proud of myself.
I made it, like I promised everybody. I didn't run for the comfort of a mission but slept out rough on the streets of Leeds.

Crawling out from beneath the market stall I am greeted by a smiling Simon who announces, 'Well mate, you bloody done it. Gimme that chart!'
I give him the chart my son Julian made for me and Simon laughs.
'You've already crossed today off!'
'I did it yesterday,' I reply, 'to make myself feel better. Anyhow, I've made a hour chart now. Look, 12 hours before my wife arrives.'

After cleaning my teeth in that smelly toilet I said an emotional goodbye to Simon who gave me five pounds. 'Here, have a cooked breakfast today. You deserve it.'

Knowing I was soon to leave Leeds I get very hyped up and wanted to walk the mean streets alone for the last time.
Walking out the station feeling the wind in my face I start to cry, looking at those Mean Streets, thinking about the kind people I had met there.
Roaming about I held my head high. I'd beaten the rats, the wind, the rain, the disco drunks, the cold concrete floors, the dirty toilets the loneliness, the emptiness.

'I've done it !' I shouted out loud.

'A day at a time without drink or drugs. I f--ing well did it !'

Quietly I crept behind Marks and Spencer's where Macca was asleep looking like a baby, so peaceful.

'Goodbye, my friend. Thanks for offering me your Swiss roll,' I whispered.

Now it was over to the Bus Shelter where Ronny and Richard were sitting on the radiator half awake, half asleep. I said goodbye to them, then went off in search of Tim.

At the warehouse I searched for him from room to room but found nobody. The rats were still there, mind.

Back outside I became more and more emotional, screaming out loud, 'My Mean Streets, my bloody Mean Streets!'

Round and round Leeds I walked, having got to know every crack in those pavements.

7 a.m. With Simon's five pounds I'm heading for the little cafe behind the station with its neon sign. I order my breakfast and sitting down to eat my fry-up see a man looking more weather-beaten

The rooftops of Leeds.

that any I'd ever seen sit opposite me. He is short with matted brown hair and a long beard. His face is creased with years of hard living. Wearing a dirty donkey jacket he looks a typical hobo. Because he doesn't have a tea or anything in front of him I push my breakfast over to him and order another for myself.

Staring at me he says, 'I know you from the old days, you slept at the Crypt, didn't you?'

He looks just like any other old tramp to me but he clearly remembers me.

'Remember Big Fat John? He had a heart attack,' he says, staring at me.
I don't recall Big Fat John but I suddenly remember many of the other tramps he starts talking about.
The more he keeps on, the more it all comes back to me.
'Danni Oppi died,' he continues.
'Scoucer's dead and old Andrew Skellet jumped off a bridge and survived. Three years later they found him unconscious on beer and wine in a house but saved him again. A month after that he burnt to death drunk. Don Patterson died, too.'
I listen with amazement and suddenly the man in front of me seems familiar.
'What's your name?' I ask him.
'John Walsh,' he replies.
'Remember the marmite at tea time?' Now I can clearly see us both as young men in our thirties, queuing up for our tea.
'Yes, I remember you, now!' I reply and reach out for his hand.
'John, what happened to you?'

'Drink, that's my problem,' he says with a far-away look as he goes on to describe the chaotic years since we'd last met.
'Drink was my problem, too,' I say, 'and drugs, but I've got off it all.'

'How?' he asks.

I go on to tell him how I had met Hannelore while I was living in the gutter and how I now attend Alcoholics Anonymous meetings regularly.
He listens intently.
I tell him exactly why I was in Leeds and that my wife was flying over from Munich today to be reunited with me in a few hour's time.
'I want to show you something' he says, producing a beautiful cigarette lighter from his pocket. 'Nice isn't it?'
'Very,' I reply.
'Take it Steve, as a present from someone from the old days.
Go back to Munich. The mission days are over for you!'

For twenty years I had lived with the fear of returning to the gutter. The thought haunted me every day. Now it was gone.
Those words of John Walsh freed me!
I arranged to meet John later that morning but sadly he never showed up so I spent the morning talking with Father Nick. Later I met the BBC film crew in the city square as arranged to wait for Hannelore.

2 p.m. 'She's walking over from the station now,' the cameraman announces. 'Your wife's here.'

The cigarette lighter John Walsh, my friend from twenty years ago, gave me.

Seeing Hannelore walking towards me I am overcome and run over to her. We don't say anything but just hug each other.

'Kept you safe,' she says, touching the medallion.

I just smile.

'Let me show you Hellhole Hotel' I insist.
After looking around a bit we are taken by taxi to the BBC studios.

Then we watch the documentary together and are both very moved by it.
'Just got to add on the reunion and film the two of you leaving by train,' one of the producers explains.
A short while later I introduce Hannelore to Father Nick, saying, 'Without this man I would never have made it.'
Unfortunately there isn't much time and we have to get back in the taxi to rush to the station.
As we hold hands in the cab I look out the window to see Macca at the corner.
I wave but he doesn't see me.
'Who was that?' my wife asks.
'The nicest person I ever met,' I reply.

The station looks so different now. It's daytime and Simon isn't there, nor Suzie, the night cleaner.

I quickly go down to the toilet where I'd washed every day to take one last look.

As we are being filmed getting on the train it starts to snow.

Roger and Patrick, the producers, smile and wave goodbye as the train pulls out.

It is all over.

On the train I sob my heart out thinking of all the people I left behind on the Mean Streets of Leeds - Mick, Macca, Tim, Ronny and Richard and Old Tom and so many more.
I also think about Simon, Suzie, Father Nick, the BBC crew Patrick, Roger and John as well as Chris and Alex, the students who took the photos.

In London my agent meets us at Kings Cross Station and takes us to a friend's house. That night I feel terribly disorientated and keep waking up. It isn't out of fear, though.

The words of John Walsh, my old tramp friend I'd met in the cafe, are ringing in my ear.

'The mission days are over for you.'

For me they are.

But sadly, for so many others they never end!

Back with Hannelore.

DAY SEVENTEEN
Thursday, December 18th

Spent the entire day at Broadcasting House, giving radio interviews by link-up to towns all over England and found it very exhausting.

I read the Daily Express interview and as I always believed found Cheryl had done a wonderful job!

I can't stop thinking of Macca and all the others.

DAY EIGHTEEN
Friday, December 19th

7 a.m. The day started early with an EBN Live TV interview.

9 a.m. All morning I was busy with the 'London Tonight' television interview. I was filmed as a tramp on the streets of London and found the whole thing quite touching.

Interviewed by The Guardian Newspaper.

Every time I passed someone begging in the street I stopped. There are far more down-and-outs down here than up in Leeds. They are on every street corner!
12 a.m. The Sybil Ruscoe interview for Radio 5 was wonderful. I like that woman.

The BBC live interview on TV went well, too.

Now it was time to take a car over to Downing Street where at 1 p.m. Hannelore and myself delivered the letter I wrote to Tony Blair on the streets of Leeds to the door of Number 10.

4 p.m. Ray Adamson, the Lord Mayor of Camden, hosted a launch party for 'Mean Street Diaries' and laid on a super buffet. Hannelore gave some press and television interviews regarding my past and her views about our relationship.

Later that day I had an emotional reunion with my grown-up daughters who were relieved to see me safe and well.

Presenting a petition on behalf of all the homeless to Mr. Blair.

Me with Ray Adamson, the Mayor of Camden, at book launch.

DAY NINETEEN
Saturday, December 20th

I gave radio interviews all day again. It was quite exhausting!

Spent the evening alone walking around the Bull Ring at Waterloo and met some down-and-out friends again.

Leeds, London, Liverpool - it's the same everywhere on skid row.

DAY TWENTY
Sunday, December 21st

Gave radio interviews again.

Read the Observer Article by Lucy Johnston. It was great and I was very pleased.

DAY TWENTY ONE
Monday, December 22nd

Another day giving radio interviews. The best interview of all was with Andrea Oliver on GLR.
I found the feedback from callers all over the country very touching. There is a lot of feeling out there for the homeless. People want to help.

DAY TWENTY TWO
Tuesday, December 23rd

6 a.m. Left for Southampton for an interview on the Espresso Show on Channel Five TV.

4 p.m. Hannelore and I met at Heathrow to fly home together to be with our sons at Christmas in Germany.

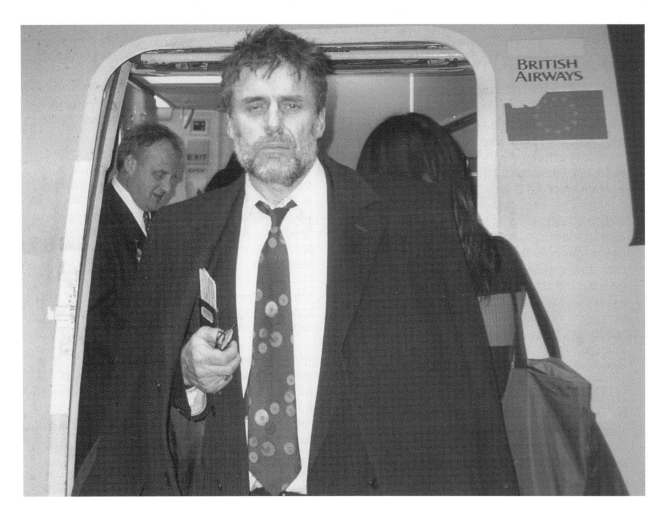

Exhausted I get the plane home.

CONCLUSION

My stay in Leeds has deepened my gratitude for being free from the clutches of addiction one day at a time. Many times over those seventeen days I found it hard to believe that I myself once was so ill to have lived like that.

Alcohol and drug addiction is an illness and I feel blessed to have found a programme, a guide to living, which helps me lead a happy and full life without the crutches of booze or drugs. Life can be extremely frightening at times but my stay in Leeds has shown me that, by facing reality head-on and confronting what is, you can't get to the other side drink and drug free.

By the time people come to sleep in a shop doorway they have gone downhill for many years. Many (though not all) are addicted and their judgement becomes clouded.

Like myself years ago a person on skid row needs a long period of on-going therapy and help if they are to become a functioning member of society again. You cannot take a meths drinker and say to him, 'Pull yourself together, get yourself cleaned up and look for work.'

They need somewhere to live. Not a dormitory where fifty men are all sleeping crowded together. We must provide accommodation which offers some form of dignity and freedom.

After giving them a roof over their heads they need further guidance to develop an interest in something that later-on could lead to some form of training scheme.

Training is vital to the recovery process of each and every homeless person because it provides a daily routine, a time to get up, a place to go to. A time to start and a time to finish. It marks the difference between weekdays and the free time at weekends.

On skid row every day is the same and it is essential to acquaint the ex-tramp with order and stability again.

The first years after coming out of the gutter were very hard for me. I had to force myself to do the most mundane things like taking baths, making my bed, folding my clothes. It took time for me to learn how to live without drugs and drink.

When Hannelore met me all those years ago I was a hopeless case everybody else had given up on. Through her faith and love I clawed my way back to life - inch by inch, day by day.

Let us show the same love to those still down there and reach out to help them back.

Nobody was born a tramp !

Together again.

Alex and Chris, the students
who took the photos.

The village where I live.